Text by Frederick C. Klein

For the Love of the Yankees

An A-to-Z Primer for Yankees Fans of All Ages

Illustrations by Mark Anderson

This book of great Yankees,
In verses that rhyme,
Tells why we're remembered,
And will be for all time.

Though I didn't pick them,
I know and can say
The selection's terrific.
I saw most of 'em play.

There's one named DiMaggio,
Another called Ruth.
To say they're deserving
Is no stretch of the truth.

If you look for some others,
    Their names might be missing.
Opinions may vary:
    Some cheering, some hissing!

So as to who's here,
I yield to my betters.
    It's only too bad
We've just 26 letters!

—Yogi Berra

"A" is for A-Rod,

Who joined the Bronx heroes
With a contract containing
A whole lot of zeroes.

ALEX RODRIGUEZ BECAME THE HIGHEST-PAID BASEBALL PLAYER EVER when he jumped from the Seattle Mariners to the Texas Rangers in December 2000 for a contract worth $252 million over 10 years. A shortstop who was an excellent hitter, he starred for the Rangers, hitting 156 homers and driving in 395 runs in three seasons with them, but the team won no titles and sought to trade him. The Yankees responded. Playing third base in New York, his power numbers (36 home runs, 106 RBIs) didn't match his annual Texas output, but he was a valuable member of the 2004 divisional champs.

"B" is for Yogi Berra,

Who was a great catch.

With a bat–or a quote–

He had hardly a match.

LAWRENCE "YOGI" BERRA WAS THE YANKEES' CATCHER from 1947 through 1963, a span that included 14 American League pennants and 10 World Series titles. He was the American League Most Valuable Player three times and was selected as an All-Star 15 times. After his playing days he managed the 1964 pennant-winning team, and became known for unintentionally funny lines such as "You can see a lot just by observing."

"C" is for Roger Clemens,

Who scattered the hitters
With fastballs that gave
Even catchers the jitters.

ROGER CLEMENS, A RIGHT-HANDED PITCHER WHO STANDS 6'4" AND WEIGHS 235 POUNDS, came to the Yankees in a 1999 trade and anchored a starting staff that won three straight pennants. His 98-mph fastballs and split-finger delivery have made this Texas native one of the game's all-time strikeout leaders.

"D" is for Joe DiMaggio,

Whom all fans embrace–
The sleek "Yankee Clipper,"
Whose trademark was grace.

JOE DIMAGGIO WAS THE YANKEES' CENTER FIELDER from 1936 through 1951 except during three years of World War II military service. A .325 lifetime hitter and the holder of baseball's consecutive-game hitting record (56, set in 1941), he was known almost equally for his powerful throwing arm and his skill and range in the field.

"E" is for Eddie Lopat;
This lefty was able.
With Reynolds and Raschi,
The Yanks ran the table.

"STEADY" EDDIE LOPAT WAS A CRAFTY LEFT-HANDED PITCHER who performed for the Yankees from 1948 through 1955. With power-throwing right-handers Allie Reynolds and Vic Raschi, he was part of a starting rotation that dominated baseball during that era.

"F" is for Whitey Ford,

A pitcher with guile.

His 10 Series wins

Were done in high style.

EDWARD "WHITEY" FORD, A LEFT-HANDER, WAS THE YANKEES' PITCHING ACE from the mid fifties through the early sixties. His lifetime winning percentage of .690 (236–106) is the best of any 20th century hurler. The record-holder for World Series pitching victories (10), he once pitched 33 consecutive scoreless innings in Series games.

"G" is for Lou Gehrig,

Who knew only one way:

The great "Iron Horse"

Came to play every day.

LOU GEHRIG WAS THE POWER-HITTING FIRST BASEMAN on the great Yankee teams of the twenties and thirties. He batted fourth in the team's lineup, and wore No. 4, just behind Babe Ruth, who wore 3. Gehrig was a .340 lifetime hitter and had 100 or more RBIs in 13 straight seasons. His consecutive-game streak of 2,130 was a record for many years, and led to his "Iron Horse" nickname.

"H" is for Elston Howard,

Who played in a mask.

For 13 seasons

He was up to the task.

IN 1955 ELSTON HOWARD BECAME THE FIRST African American to play for the Yankees. He succeeded Yogi Berra as starting catcher, and played on nine pennant-winning teams before retiring in 1967. He was a frequent All-Star, and was named American League Most Valuable Player in 1963.

"I" is for innings.

The standard is nine.
But if the game's tied,
Then more are just fine.

"J" is for Jackson and Jeter,

Two guys you could love.

Reggie beat 'em with muscle;

Derek won with his glove.

REGGIE JACKSON WAS A LEFT-HANDED-HITTING SLUGGER who led the champion Yankee teams of 1977, 1978, and 1981. His World Series exploits earned him the nickname "Mr. October." Derek Jeter was a Rookie-of-the-Year short-stop in 1996 at age 22, and went on to achieve All-Star status in five of his first seven seasons. Also a potent hitter, he shows promise of becoming the best Yankee ever at his position.

"K" is for "Wee" Willie Keeler,

A true baseball saint.

He was the guy who

"Hit 'em where they ain't."

"WEE" WILLIE KEELER WAS ONE OF THE STARS OF BASEBALL'S HIGH-COLLAR ERA, playing from 1892 through 1910. Seven of those seasons (1903–1909) were with the Yankees. Small in stature (he stood 5'4½"), this left-hander was the model slap hitter, consistently aiming singles through infield holes. He had 2,932 career hits and a lifetime batting average of .341.

Zero

"L" is for Don Larsen,

A World Series hero.
He mowed down the Dodgers
With nothing but zeros.

DON LARSEN WAS A JOURNEYMAN PITCHER who had more career losses than wins, but on October 8, 1956, he threw the only perfect game in World Series history, beating the Brooklyn Dodgers 2–0. He had stayed out late the night before, but told a newspaper reporter who saw him return to his hotel that he would pitch a no-hitter anyway.

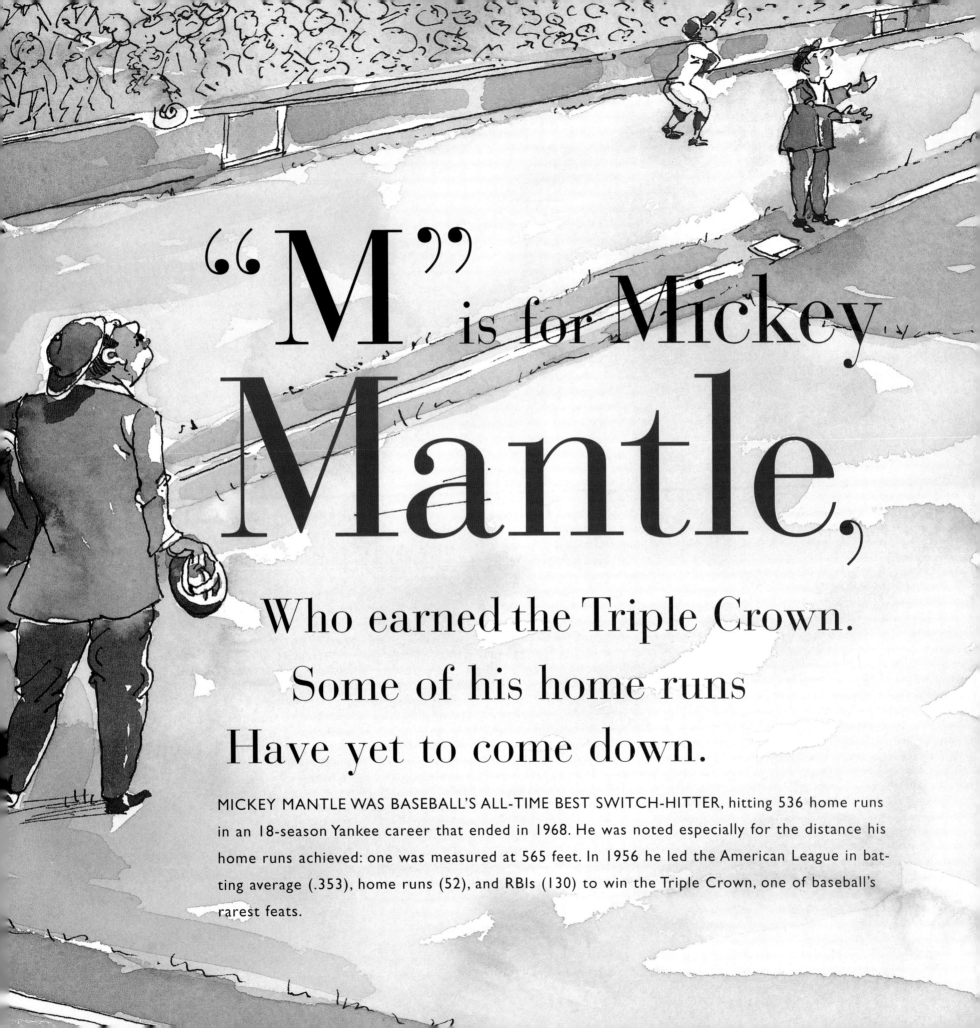

"M" is for Mickey Mantle,

Who earned the Triple Crown.
Some of his home runs
Have yet to come down.

MICKEY MANTLE WAS BASEBALL'S ALL-TIME BEST SWITCH-HITTER, hitting 536 home runs in an 18-season Yankee career that ended in 1968. He was noted especially for the distance his home runs achieved: one was measured at 565 feet. In 1956 he led the American League in batting average (.353), home runs (52), and RBIs (130) to win the Triple Crown, one of baseball's rarest feats.

"N" is for Graig Nettles,
Who without any doubt
Changed many a line drive
From double to out.

GRAIG NETTLES PLAYED THIRD BASE
for the Yankees from 1973 through 1983, and
while he hit with power (he had 390 career home
runs), he was best known for his fielding
prowess. He was a five-time American
League All-Star.

PAUL O'NEILL PLAYED OUTFIELD,
first base, and designated hitter for
the pennant-winning Yankees of the
1996–2001 period. He was never a
star, but was respected for his steady
production in the middle of the batting order. He averaged 95 RBIs a
year during his nine seasons with the
team.

"O" is for O'Neill,
Who had just the right touch.
With runners on base
He came through in the clutch.

"P" is for poor Wally Pipp,

Who had a headache one day.
That was the last time
The Yankees let him play.

WALLY PIPP HAD A LONG AND HONORABLE major league
career, but is best known for surrendering his job as first baseman
to rookie Lou Gehrig early in the 1925 season. Veterans who are
replaced in their lineups by promising rookies are still
compared with Pipp.

"Q" is for the quest:

A pennant each year.
If the Yankees don't win it,
They get a Bronx cheer.

"R" is for Ruth,

The "Sultan of Swat,"

"The Babe," "The Bambino,"

Who once called his shot.

GEORGE HERMAN "BABE" RUTH WAS, IN THE OPINION OF MANY, the greatest baseball player of all time. He began his career as a pitcher for the Boston Red Sox, and excelled in that capacity. After his 1920 trade to the Yankees he was switched to the outfield because of his hitting prowess. He went on to set records for most home runs in a season (60) and career home runs (714), both of which stood for many years. It is said that on October 1, 1932, in a World Series game against the Chicago Cubs, he pointed to center field and then hit a home run to the same spot. Many people question whether he really "called his shot," but the incident is part of baseball lore.

"S" is for Stengel;

The lineups he'd juggle.

His teams won 10 pennants

Without too much struggle.

CHARLES DILLON "CASEY" STENGEL HAD THE MOST REMARKABLE run of any baseball manager in history, with 10 pennants and seven World Series titles in his 12 seasons with the team (1949–1960). He also amused and perplexed fans with his imaginative use of the English language.

"T" is for Joe Torre,

The man in the wings.
Through four Series triumphs
He pulled the right strings.

JOE TORRE HAS BEEN ANOTHER GREAT YANKEE MANAGER, guiding the 1996, 1998, 1999, and 2000 World Series–winning teams. A quiet and gentlemanly person, he was credited with bringing purpose and unity to a roster brimming with individualistic and highly paid players.

"U" is for the "Big Unit."

Nearly seven feet tall,
To batters it seems
He's handing catchers the ball.

RANDY JOHNSON CAME TO THE YANKEES IN TRADE after the 2004 season as one of baseball's all-time strikeout leaders, having fanned 4,161 in a 17-year career with four major league teams. Standing 6'10", the long-armed lefty's fastball and breaking pitches seem to explode upon hitters, sending them back to the bench shaking their heads in frustration. Ironically, his brightest moments came against the Yankees in the 2001 World Series, where he won three games and posted a 1.04 ERA in leading the Arizona Diamondbacks to their first championship.

"V" is for victories

And titles galore. In all baseball's history
No team has won more.

FROM THEIR FOUNDING AS THE NEW YORK HIGHLANDERS IN 1903 THROUGH 2002, the Yankees won 38 American League pennants and 26 World Series titles, both baseball highs. Their .568 regular-season victory percentage (8,777 wins, 6,687 losses) also ranked first. They are among the most successful franchises of any sport in any country.

"W" is for Williams, and Winfield, and White.

They gave their teams' lineups
Plenty of bite.

BERNIE WILLIAMS, WHO IS ORIGINALLY FROM PUERTO RICO, has been the star center fielder on the Yankee teams of the late nineties and early 21st century. Dave Winfield, a power-hitting outfielder, got 1,300 of his 3,110 career hits during his 1981–1990 tenure with the team. Outfielder Roy White was a consistently productive player over his 15-year Yankee career (1965–1979).

"X" marks the spot
Of the longest home run.

It was hit by a **Tiger**
Whose first name was Juan.

THE LONGEST HOME RUN HIT IN YANKEE STADIUM since it was remodeled during 1976 was a 470-foot blast into the left-field bleachers hit by Juan Encarnacion of the Detroit Tigers on July 24, 2001. The Yanks' Mickey Mantle hit a home run to center field in a 1964 game that was estimated to have traveled about that far.

"Y" is for Yankee Stadium,
The best in the land.
When "the Babe" built a house,
He built it to stand.

YANKEE STADIUM, LOCATED IN THE NEW YORK BOROUGH OF THE BRONX, was dubbed "the House that Ruth Built" when it was opened in 1923. It is baseball's best-known field as well as its third oldest, behind only Fenway Park in Boston and Wrigley Field in Chicago. Yankee Stadium has been renovated several times; the most extensive changes were part of a two-year project that was completed in 1976. The stadium can now seat 57,478 people.

"Z" is for Tom Zachary,

Who changed in midstream.
He served up Babe's 60th
And then joined the team.

TOM ZACHARY WAS THE PITCHER WHO, as a Washington Senator, was on the mound when Babe Ruth hit his record-setting 60th home run on the last day of the 1927 season. He was traded to the Yankees the next year, and posted a 12–0 record for the 1929 club.

When it comes to the Yankees,
The alphabet fetters.
There are too many names
And not enough letters.

What book, for example,
Could leave out Crosetti,
Bill Dickey, Rizzuto,
Or big Dave Righetti?

Add Jim Hunter, Red Ruffing,
Rich Gossage ("The Goose"),
Ron Guidry, Tom Heinrich,
And Bill Skowron ("The Moose").

Maris and Mattingly,
Martin and Munson;
Just "M" guys could fill
This whole book—and then some!

Miller Huggins could manage,
    And McCarthy, when it counted.
With Houk in the dugout,
    The title toll mounted.

And don't forget George–
    That's Steinbrenner, the Boss.
We can't leave him out,
    Or he's apt to be cross.

The list could go on,
    But we'll cut it off here.
We need to leave room
    For new heroes to cheer!

–The End

"A" is for Mel Allen

"B" is for Yogi Berra

"C" is for Roger Clemens

"D" is for Joe DiMaggio

"E" is for Eddie Lopat

"F" is for Whitey Ford

"G" is for Lou Gehrig

"H" is for Elston Howard

"J" is for Reggie Jackson and
Derek Jeter

"K" is for "Wee" Willie Keeler

"L" is for Don Larsen

"M" is for Mickey Mantle

"N" is for Graig Nettles

"P" is for Wally Pipp

"R" is for Babe Ruth

"S" is for Casey Stengel

"T" is for Joe Torre

"W" is for Bernie Williams,
Dave Winfield, and Roy White

"X" marks the spot of the
longest home run

"Y" is for Yankee Stadium

"Z" is for Tom Zachary

Library of Congress Control Number: 2003107334

This book is available in quantity at special discounts for your group or organization.
For further information, contact:

Triumph Books
542 S. Dearborn St., Suite 750
Chicago, Illinois 60605
312. 939. 3330
Fax 312. 663. 3557

Printed in Hong Kong
ISBN-13: 978-1-57243-774-6
ISBN-10: 1-57243-774-X